Manua

ACCESS TO SHAKESPEARE

The Tragedy of
Macbeth

A Facing-pages Translation into Contemporary English

Manual for

ACCESS TO SHAKESPEARE

The Tragedy of
Macbeth

A Facing-pages Translation into Contemporary English

Jonnie Patricia Mobley, Ph.D.
Drama Department
Cuesta College
San Luis Obispo, California

Lorenz Educational Publishers
P.O. Box 146340, Chicago, IL 60614-6340

Cover border taken from the First Folio (1623)

Cover design by Tamada Brown Design, Chicago

Interior design and typesetting by David Corona Design, Dubuque

Published by Lorenz Educational Publishers. © 1999 by Lorenz Educational Publishers. PO Box 146340, Chicago, IL 60614-6340. All rights reserved. No part of this book may be reproduced, stored in a retrieval system, or transmitted in any form or by any means without the prior permission of Lorenz Educational Publishers.

ISBN: 1-885564-01-5

Library of Congress Card Catalog Number: 94-78187

Manufactured in the United States of America.

9 8 7 6 5 4 3 2

Contents

INTRODUCING SHAKESPEARE

There is an aura of unreality about the plays of Shakespeare, and students feel this although they may not be able to express their reactions precisely. They may say that Shakespeare's language is "too flowery" or that people in real life don't talk the way these characters do. And this is true. The people one meets in real life are not nearly as articulate as the characters in Shakespeare. Probably, it would be unbearable if the people one met at the bank and the supermarket, in school or during meetings spoke unrelievedly as great poets.

The characters of Shakespeare lack the reality of foggy-mindedness found in everyday life; they are concentrated and fully in command of their verbal resources. Shakespeare's is a world in which the brain and the heart and the tongue are directly connected, without the usual intervening fuzziness. It's perhaps a world that doesn't exist, but what an interesting world it is, one in which people have fully realized their potential—for good and for evil. To have imagined such a world and to have put it on paper is Shakespeare's achievement. And it is a major reason he is read and performed today.

To make that world accessible to students is the reason for this edition of *Macbeth*, a facing-pages translation with the original text on the left-hand side and a translation into contemporary English on the right. The translation of *Macbeth* is not meant to take the place of the original. After all, a translation is by its very nature a shadow of the original. The plays remain, and their substance is unaltered. This translation is an alternative to the notes usually included in modern editions. In many cases these notes interfere with the reading of the play. Whether alongside or below the original text, they break the rhythm of reading and frequently force the reader to turn back to an earlier page or jump ahead to a later one. Having a translation that runs parallel to the original, line for line, allows the reader to move easily from Elizabethan to contemporary English and back again. It's simply a better way to introduce Shakespeare.

Also, this translation is suitable for performance, where no notes are available to the audience. Admittedly, a well-directed and well-acted production can do much to clarify Shakespeare's language. And yet, there will be numerous references and lines whose meanings are not accessible on a first hearing. What, for instance, does Banquo mean when he says that he will keep his "bosom franchised"?

1

ABOUT THIS TRANSLATION

Since 1807, when Charles and Mary Lamb published *Tales from Shakespeare,* prose adaptations of Shakespeare's plays have attempted, more or less success- fully, to broaden the audience for these plays—or perhaps, to restore to Shakespeare the full audience he had known in the seventeenth century. These days, prose paraphrases of the original are offered to students. Insofar as they succeed, these paraphrases offer a kind of literal rendering of the original, largely stripped of metaphor and poetry. To read them by themselves, without reference to the original, would make you wonder why Shakespeare is still popular.

The translation in this edition aims to retain the feel and the rhythm of the original, but at the same time to be immediately comprehensible to modern audiences and readers, so that they can experience Shakespeare in much the same way the Elizabethans did. That means preserving the sound and the spirit of the original.

Here, for example is a passage taken from the last act of *Macbeth.* His world has become unhinged. One of the officers in the opposing army describes Macbeth's situation:

> Now does he feel
> His secret murders sticking on his hands;
> Now minutely revolts upbraid his faith-breach;
> Those he commands move only in command,
> Nothing in love. Now does he feel his title
> Hang loose about him, like a giant's robe
> Upon a dwarfish thief.

The first two lines are as colorful and clear to a modern audience as they were four hundred years ago to the Elizabethans. The trouble begins in line 3. *Minutely* no longer means "every minute" but "in a small quantity." A modern reader might readily interpret this line as, "a small quantity of revolts upbraid his faith-breach." And the phrase "upbraid his faith-breach" is not current idiom, thus compounding the problem. Line 4 might be interpreted to mean that his troops are obedient, which is not what an Elizabethan audience understood. "Nothing in love" in line 5, which to Elizabethans meant "not from love" remains opaque to many modern English-speakers.

To be effective and authentic, a translation into contemporary English should not only be immediately clear, but retain the ring of Shakespeare. The original and the modified parts should meld so seamlessly that, if you did not have the original at hand, you might think you were reading it.

> Now does he feel
> His secret murders sticking on his hands;

Every minute rebellions reproach his treachery.
Those he commands move only because they're ordered,
Not from love. Now does he feel his title
Hang loose about him, like a giant's robe
Upon a dwarfish thief.

Here, for comparison, is another approach to translating Shakespeare. Although clear to a modern reader, it does not have the feel and the sound of Shakespeare.

Now his hidden murders
Are returning to haunt him.
Rebellions multiply against his seizure of the throne.
His troops fight only because they are commanded to do so,
Not because they support him. Now he feels his royal title
Draped loosely about him, hanging like a giant's robe
On a dwarfish thief.

This second translation is contemporary, not only in vocabulary, but in sound and style. It is not Shakespearean in spirit.

Take another example. It is from Act Four of the original text. A Scottish noble, in exile in England, asks a recent arrival about the situation in Scotland. The reply is as follows:

Alas, poor country,
Almost afraid to know itself. It cannot
Be called our mother, but our grave; where nothing
But who knows nothing, is once seen to smile;
Where sighs and groans, and shrieks that rent the air,
Are made, not marked; where violent sorrow seems
A modern ecstasy. The dead man's knell
Is there scarce asked for who, and good men's lives
Expire before the flowers in their caps,
Dying or ere they sicken.

The student comes away from this passage with the general impression that things are pretty bad in Scotland. But he or she may be baffled by the details. The translation supplies the details clearly.

Ah, poor country,
Almost afraid to know itself. You cannot
Call it our mother now, but our grave, where no one
But those who know nothing could smile;
Where sighs and groans and shrieks that tear the air

Pass unnoticed; where violent sorrow has become
A common emotion. The tolling of funeral bells
Prompts no one to ask for whom, and good men's lives
Expire before the flowers in their caps,
Killed off before they wither.

LINE COUNTS

Scholars of Shakespeare, following the precedent of the *Globe* edition, number the lines of verse. When they find two short lines in a row, as often happens when speakers in a play change, they count these two short lines as one. Similarly, when a line is too long to fit in the column and has to be run over, scholars count these two lines of type as one line of verse. As the British scholar G. B. Harrison explains it:

> In *Macbeth*, for instance, the Folio text sometimes prints short lines of verse. Editors have often joined them to make complete blank-verse lines, rearranging the rest of the speech. Shakespeare sometimes began a blank-verse speech with a half-line. This irritated editors, who shift the lines up to make them look better, until they come to some line that cannot be shifted. Then they leave it as a broken line and start again.

What's more, as Harrison goes on to point out, "Much of *Macbeth* is not written in formal blank verse at all, but in a kind of rhythmic verse."

Consistency breaks down completely when it comes to counting lines of prose. With prose, the lines are numbered as they occur on the page.

These methods of lineation, as it is called, have several advantages for scholars, but they can be confusing to students. To them, a line means a line of type, not a line of verse. So, if you are using a conventional text, and you ask students to look at line 18, that line could be the seventeenth line of type from the beginning of the scene or the nineteenth. In this edition of *Macbeth,* every line of type is counted, short or runover, and every fifth line is numbered in the margin. Scene descriptions and stage directions are, of course, excluded from the count. With this system, you can be sure that you and your students are looking at the same line in the text.

SOURCE OF THE PLAY

There was a real Macbeth, and he ruled Scotland from 1040 to 1057. His story was told by Raphael Holinshed in his *Chronicles of England, Scotland, and Ireland.* According to Holinshed, Macbeth killed Duncan to seize the throne and was in turn killed by the son of the king he had dispossessed. The 1587 edition of this work served as the source of the plot for Shakespeare's play. Shakespeare, however, did not feel bound to follow Holinshed in depicting either the events or the personalities of the people described in the *Chronicles.* In Holinshed, King Duncan is described as a weak and cowardly ruler, and he is killed in open combat, not in his sleep. (The assassination by stealth was taken from a different story in Holinshed, the murder of King Duff.) Banquo is Macbeth's accomplice. Lady Macbeth is mentioned only once by Holinshed. Macbeth is promised the throne by the "weird sisters," but the ambiguous prophecies on which Macbeth relies as the play progresses are made by "certain wizards" and a witch.

Holinshed, moreover, provides Macbeth with some legitimate claim to the throne. According to Scottish law, the throne passed to the next in blood to the king if the king died before his eldest son came of age. By naming Malcolm the Prince of Cumberland, Duncan was in effect depriving Macbeth of his right to succession. Shakespeare ignores this circumstance in creating his play.

According to Holinshed, the first ten years of Macbeth's rule were wise and just, in which Macbeth "set his whole intention to maintain justice and to punish all enormities and abuses." Only later, brooding on the fact that he has no heirs and that Banquo's line would succeed to the throne, does Macbeth turn into a tyrant.

In transforming his source, Shakespeare has produced his most original tragedy, telescoping time and concentrating the dramatic effects—producing a play with a tightly woven pattern.

SHAKESPEARE'S LIFE

No one knows exactly when William Shakespeare was born. What is known is that he was baptized on April 26, 1564, in the Holy Trinity Church at Stratford-upon- Avon, a small town less than a hundred miles from London. He was the third child of John and Mary Shakespeare. He probably attended, beginning at age four or five, the King's New School in Stratford. The school was one of the so-called grammar schools established to teach young men to read and write and, after two years, to study Latin grammar and literature. Since the records of the school have not survived, it cannot be proven that Shakespeare was actually enrolled there. There is a record, however, in 1582 of Shakespeare's marriage to Anne Hathaway. He was eighteen at the time and she was twenty-six. Their first child, Susanna, was born in 1583, and twins, Judith and Hamnet, were born two years later.

Between then and 1592 Shakespeare left Stratford and established himself in the world of London theatre. In that year the playwright Robert Greene published a book in which he attacked a certain actor who had the audacity to write blank-verse plays. This actor, "an upstart crow," was "in his own conceit the onely Shake-scene in a country." The actor had aroused Greene's ire by successfully competing against university-educated dramatists like Greene himself.

Also in 1592 Shakespeare became a published poet with his narrative poem *Venus and Adonis*. Another poem, *The Rape of Lucrece,* was published the following year. Both poems were dedicated to the Earl of Southampton, a wealthy patron of the arts, whom Shakespeare no doubt knew and liked.

When the London theaters reopened in 1594, after having been closed to curb the spread of a deadly plague, Shakespeare resumed his dual career as actor and dramatist. By now he was also a shareholder in his company, the Lord Chamberlain's Men, later named the King's Men. In 1599 Shakespeare's company built their own theater on the other side of the Thames River, across from London. Shakespeare apparently prospered and invested his income in real estate in London and Stratford. Sometime between 1610 and 1613, he returned to Stratford and retired.

On April 23, 1616, he died and was buried two days later within the chancel of Holy Trinity Church. The inscription on his stone in Holy Trinity Church reads as follows:

Good friend, for Jesus' sake, forbear
To dig the dust enclosed here;
Blest be the man that spares these stones
And cursed be he who moves my bones.

Several years after his death, in 1623, two members of Shakespeare's company, John Heminge and Henry Condell, collected his plays and published them in what has become known as the First Folio. Previous to this, Shakespeare's plays were sometimes published individually in quartos. (A quarto is a sheet of paper folded in half twice, yielding four leaves, or eight pages of type, whereas a folio is folded in half once, yielding two leaves, or four pages of type.)

Shakespeare's last direct descendant, his granddaughter, Elizabeth Hall, died in 1670.

SHAKESPEARE'S LANGUAGE

Shakespeare's language does present problems for modern readers. After all, four centuries of change have intervened. During this time many words have acquired new meanings or were dropped from the language altogether; spelling and sentence structures have become less fluid. But these problems are solvable.

First of all, most of the words that Shakespeare used are still current. For those words whose meanings have changed and for those no longer in the language, modern equivalents are found in this translation. For a small number of words—chiefly, names of places, biblical and mythological characters, and formal titles—a glossary can be found on page 183 of the text of the play. Another glossary will be found in the manual on page 39.

The meaning of words is one problem. The position of words is another. Today, the order of words in declarative sentences is almost fixed. First comes the subject, then the verb, and finally, when there is one, the object. In Shakespeare's time, the order of words, particularly in poetic drama was more flexible. Shakespeare has Macbeth say,

So foul and fair a day I have not seen.

Whereas we would usually arrange the words in this order:

I have not seen so foul and fair a day.

Later in the play, Macbeth says,

Look on it again, I dare not.

We would probably say,

I dare not look on it again.

This does not mean that Shakespeare never uses words in what we consider normal order. As often as not, he does. Here, for instance, are Macbeth and Banquo in conversation.

MACBETH   Your children shall be kings.
BANQUO   You shall be king.

When Shakespeare inverts the order of words, he does so for a variety of reasons—to create a rhythm, to emphasize a word, to achieve a rhyme. Whether a play is in verse, as most of this play is, or in prose, it is still written in sentences. And this means that, despite the order, all the words needed to make complete sentences are there. If your students are puzzled by a sentence, tell them to first look for the subject and then try rearranging the words in the order they would normally use. It takes a little practice, but they will be surprised how quickly they acquire the skill.

Shakespeare sometimes separates sentence parts—subject and verb, for example—that would normally be run together. Here are some lines describing Macbeth in battle,

For brave Macbeth—well he deserves that name—
Disdaining Fortune with his brandished steel,
Which smoked with bloody execution,
Like Valor's darling, carved out his path.

Between the subject, *Macbeth,* and the verb, *carved out,* come some clauses and phrases that interrupt the normal sequence. Again, have your students look for the subject and then the verb and put the two together. The rearranged sentence, though clear, will probably not be as rhythmical as Shakespeare's.

SHAKESPEARE'S THEATRE

When most people think of a theatre building, they picture the proscenium arch auditorium, but, of course, there are other types: the thrust stage, the black box (a room painted and draped entirely in black), and the "found space" of a converted cafeteria or campus quad. The closest to Shakespeare's theatre, the "Wooden O" of the Globe Theatre, is the present-day arena theatre where the audience surrounds the stage. The Globe, where most of Shakespeare's plays were originally produced, was a circular or polygonal wooden structure of galleries surrounding an open courtyard area. Centered near one side of this courtyard was a covered wooden platform. Immediately in front of this platform was the area designated the "pit" (much later it became our modern orchestra pit, and the seats sold as orchestra seats) where the groundlings stood—the rowdy, uneducated rabble who paid a small fee to attend a play. (The low comedy elements in Shakespeare's plays were directed toward them.) Patrons who could afford it, paid more and sat in the surrounding galleries or even on the stage itself.

Most of the play's action took place on the platform itself. At the rear of the platform was a curtained alcove which could be used to represent an inner room or a tomb, depending on the needs of the play. On the second level, above the alcove, the area, uncurtained, could serve to represent a bed chamber or balcony. The third level of this back wall could serve as yet another setting but was more often where the musicians sat.

The fourth level was closed off from the audience and from there came the sound effects such as the bell ringing in *Macbeth.* The platform had trap doors. Right and left of the main stage area were tiring rooms, short for retiring, where the actors could dress.

There were no curtains to conceal the main stage from the audience, so plays flowed from scene to scene without interruption, perhaps only the slightest pause or brief musical interlude to indicate a change of time or place.

Because the Globe was open to the air, performances could utilize the natural illumination of daylight, although torches were also used, when necessary. The whole structure of the Globe and other theatres that imitated it, reminds us of the yards of inns where the first traveling companies of medieval actors often played.

The elaborately constructed and painted scenery that one often sees in a production of Shakespeare today was missing from the original productions. Companies were content to suggest or symbolize a setting. Several cutouts of trees could suggest a forest; a few rocks, the entrance to a castle; or a banner on a pole, the throne room of King Duncan.

There was sparing use of props, but some are documented in a list of stage properties kept by Philip Henslowe, the Elizabethan theatre magnate. The production of *Macbeth* calls for such items as a table, seats of some kind, and a cauldron.

Costumes were not as lavish as in many modern productions, but the leading players were certainly dressed appropriately in armor, court clothing, or night-dress. By the eighteenth century, there was attention paid to the authenticity of the clan tartans, or plaids, worn in *Macbeth,* but at least one production earned a bad review in a theatrical publication of the time for having Macbeth and Banquo dressed in silken hose and powdered hair as they encountered the witches on the blasted heath.

There were no women in the theatre companies of Shakespeare's time. All the parts were played by men and the boys who were apprentices in the company. As one looks at the cast lists for the plays, it is easy to see that the male characters outnumber the women, and for a very practical reason. The women's parts that do exist, however, offer actors wonderful opportunities.

The repertory system for theatrical companies came into being with the construction of permanent theatre buildings in London. In order to keep attracting an audience to their plays, the companies had to change their offerings frequently. In a two-week period a company might offer as many as ten different plays in rotation. An actor with the lead in one play would be expected to take a minor role in the next play, perhaps have a break from the third play, and again appear in a minor role for the next play, and then once again play a lead in the fifth play. As new plays were introduced into the repertoire, actors found themselves rehearsing a new play while still performing in an older one. Actors in repertory companies needed physical stamina, versatility in acting, and had to be quick studies—that is, fast at learning lines.

STAGE DIRECTIONS

In drama written for the modern stage, the playwright provides detailed directions for the actors—how to move and speak, what emotions to convey to an audience. In the plays of Shakespeare, stage directions are sparse. One reason for this could be that Shakespeare was a member and an owner of the company for which he wrote these plays. He was there to tell the other actors how to say a line or what gesture to use. Even so, the dialogue itself offers clues to actions and gestures. For example, Macbeth, in Act Two, imagines he sees a dagger in the air in front of him. He says,

> I see you still, in a form as palpable
> As this which now I draw.

At this point, Macbeth probably draws a real dagger.

Again, in Act One, Lady Macbeth greets Duncan at the entrance of her castle. Duncan says,

> By your leave, hostess.

And they enter the castle. At this point, Duncan may take Lady Macbeth's arm or possibly give her a kiss. The line calls for some gesture but, of course, lacking a written direction, one can't be sure exactly what it is.

Remind your students that as they read, they must be alert to whom a line of dialogue is addressed. For example, after meeting the three witches who predict that Macbeth shall be king, Banquo addresses Macbeth and asks him,

> Good sir, why do you jump and seem to fear
> Things that sound so good?

Then, turning to the witches, he continues,

> In the name of truth,
> Are you a fantasy or that indeed
> Which you seem to be?

But there is no stage direction to mark this transition. Urge your students as they read to picture in their minds the characters and to decide who is talking to whom.

TRANSITIONS

Abrupt transitions occur fairly frequently in Shakespeare. Often, they are used simply to advance the plot. Often, they also reveal a psychological interplay between the characters. For example, in Act Two, Scene 2, Macbeth returns from murdering Duncan. He is upset to the point of obsession. He insists on describing to his wife the circumstances of the killing. Then he asks, "Who lies in the other room?" She replies, "Donalbain." Macbeth continues with his description. Lady

Macbeth suddenly says, "There are two roomed together." Her line is jarring and seems to make no sense. But when you remember Macbeth's earlier question about the other room and Lady Macbeth's attempt to rescue her husband from obsessive thoughts, the line makes sense. You then become aware how adroit Shakespeare is at conveying the workings of his characters' minds. The lesson here for your students is to trust Shakespeare. If a line seems at first irrelevant, don't dismiss it. Think about previous lines and see how it might fit in.

SOLO SPEECHES

There is another difference between the plays of Shakespeare and most modern ones—the solo speeches. These are the asides and the soliloquies in which a character reveals what is on his or her mind. Contemporary dramatists seem to feel that the solo speech is artificial and unrealistic. Oddly enough, modern novelists frequently use a variety of the solo speech. Some critics feel that this convention has given the novel extra power and depth, allowing writers to probe deeply into the motives of their characters. One thing is certain—Shakespeare's plays would not be as powerful as they are without the solo speeches.

TEACHING SUGGESTIONS

There are several ways in which this edition of *Macbeth* can be used with students, but perhaps the most effective is to assign a long scene or several short scenes in the translation for reading as homework. Then, in going over this material in class, use the original. This way much valuable time can be saved. Students no longer have to struggle with understanding the basic story, and you can devote your time to providing insights and in-depth appreciation of the play.

For some students, of course, the original text will still represent a formidable obstacle. In those cases, you may want to use the translation as the basis of classroom presentation with carefully selected passages from the original to illustrate the points you are making. The great advantage of this edition is its flexibility in a variety of teaching situations.

ADDITIONAL TEACHING SUGGESTIONS

Because this is a play rather than a novel or a short story with descriptive passages to provide exposition, you will probably want to discuss with your students the motivations of the various characters, their relationships with each other, and even the effects of time and place.

1. A kind of theatre game many directors use to help their actors understand the complexities of the characters in a drama like *Macbeth* is called Collage. To adapt it to classroom use, assign each student a character in *Macbeth*. It doesn't matter if more than one student has the same character as long as they don't confer. Each student must choose a color for the background—using colored paper or quickly coloring in a background. The color, of course, represents the character as the student perceives him or her. Most students are aware of the theories of colors and how they affect us, but even without such formal knowledge students are generally adept at choosing a color that suggests what their character is like.

   Next, using magazines or newspapers or even simple drawings, each student creates a collage of objects, shapes, scenery that together present all the student understands about the character he or she has been assigned. The collages are shared, one by one, with the class and the total effect of each is discussed. If two students have the same character, the result should not be a debate over who is *right* but, rather, if there are differences of opinion between the two, why did each make those particular choices of interpretation?

2. Don Eitner, a West Coast director, uses a valuable theatre game for establishing relationships within a play. He stations his actors on risers, or stairs, with the most important character at the top and the others arranged on levels according to their relationship with that character. If a character dies or is out of favor, he or she leaves the risers. As a character moves closer to the important character in the action of the play, so does the actor move closer on the risers. In the case of *Macbeth*, Duncan could stand at the top, with Malcolm immediately below.

   Macbeth and his wife could stand a little below and next to each other at first but then farther apart as events dictate. The former Thane of Cawdor, although he never appears in the play, should at first be represented in a position blocking Macbeth's passage to the throne. As the students move about and jockey for position close to the king, and after his death to the position he held, they will see the relationships of the characters in the play.

3. Turning down the thermostat in the classroom or taking field trips to desolate plains may prove impractical, but students can be made aware of the effect on characters in the play of time of year and the weather through such devices as darkening the classroom, playing tapes of thunder and storms, and showing slides of dark woods, lone plains, dank caverns, and stone castles. If they can read aloud passages from the play while experiencing such audio and visual aids, so much the better.

SUMMARIES OF ACTS AND SCENES

ACT ONE

Scene 1

This brief scene sets the tone for the play. Three witches (the Weird Sisters, as they call themselves) on a remote part of a battlefield in eleventh-century Scotland plan to meet Macbeth, a Scottish commander, when the battle is finished. (In Shakespeare's time, they would enter on a bare stage, probably through the trap door. The "fog and filthy air" would be simulated by smoke from burning resin.) The dialog of the witches suggests a world of topsy-turvy moral values in which "fair is foul and foul is fair."

Scene 2

The scene opens with a battle call on a trumpet, played off stage. A captain, bleeding from wounds he received in battle, enters the camp of King Duncan. In somewhat inflated language, he tells the king how his loyal commander Macbeth killed the rebel Macdonwald, then joined with Banquo, the other loyal commander, to fight off an attack by King Sweno of Norway. The captain is led off to have his wounds treated, and the Thane of Ross appears to continue the report. He tells how Macbeth and Banquo fought the combined troops of the Norwegian king and the traitorous Thane of Cawdor, forcing the Norwegian king to sue for a truce and pay an indemnity. Duncan directs Ross to order the execution of the Thane of Cawdor and greet Macbeth with his title.

Scene 3

The witches appear again, with thunder rolling in the background. They are plotting revenge against a sailor whose wife insulted one of them and refused to give her chestnuts. A drum announces the arrival of Macbeth, and the witches complete their spell. Macbeth and Banquo enter, Macbeth's opening line echoing a line of the witches from the first scene, "So foul and fair a day I have not seen." The witches greet Macbeth by three titles—Thane of Glamis (his present title), Thane of Cawdor (his soon-to-be title), and King. Macbeth is stunned and cannot conceal his shock from Banquo, who asks the witches to predict his future, too. They tell him that he shall father kings, although not be one himself. When Macbeth tries to question the witches further, they vanish. Ross and Angus arrive and greet Macbeth as Thane of Cawdor. Both Banquo and Macbeth are awed by how quickly one of the witches' predictions has come true. Banquo is skeptical of their motives, believing they may be an evil force. In an aside,

Macbeth faces his own fear that he had thought of murdering Duncan, but for the present he decides to leave his fate to chance. All the nobles leave to meet Duncan and his party.

Scene 4

News is brought to Duncan of the confession and execution of the former Thane of Cawdor. The king sadly admits that there is no way to know a man's mind just by looking at his face. Ironically, at that moment, Macbeth and Banquo enter with Ross and Angus. After thanking Macbeth for his heroism, Duncan declares that his own son Malcolm will be heir to the throne. Macbeth sees this as yet another obstacle in his path. When the king proposes a visit to Macbeth's castle, Inverness, Macbeth leaves to make arrangements.

Scene 5

At Inverness, Lady Macbeth reads aloud a letter from Macbeth telling her of his success in battle, his new title from the king, and the prophecies of the three witches. She determines to help her husband make the prophecies come true, feeling that he will be reluctant to do all that it might take to achieve the crown. After a messenger brings news of the king's imminent arrival, she calls on the spirits of darkness to strengthen her resolve to help Macbeth become king. Macbeth joins her, and she begins immediately to involve him in her plot against the king.

Scene 6

King Duncan and his entourage arrive at Macbeth's castle and are greeted with Lady Macbeth's insincere flattery and declarations of devotion. The king comments on the pleasant setting and sweet air of the place, not realizing the treachery that awaits him there.

Scene 7

While the others attend the banquet prepared for them, Macbeth and his wife plan the murder of the king. At Macbeth's reluctance to join her in the plot, Lady Macbeth accuses him of being less than a man and so persuades him. They plan to get Duncan's officers, or grooms, drunk, kill the king in his sleep, and smear the men with blood so they will be blamed for the murder. As the scene ends, Macbeth has agreed to everything and even adds that he and his wife must put on a friendly face to hide their evil intent, an ironic reminder that Duncan had earlier said he could not tell what was in a man's mind from looking at his face.

ACT TWO

Scene 1

After midnight, Macbeth meets Banquo and his son Fleance on their way to bed. Banquo says he has dreamed of the three witches and reminds Macbeth that part of the prophecy has already come true. Macbeth pretends indifference but suggests meeting to discuss the matter later. When he is alone, Macbeth has a vision in which a dagger hangs before him, signaling the way to the king. A bell rings and Macbeth exits to kill Duncan. The bell that Lady Macbeth has arranged as a signal rings out. It is a startling effect, and its tolling is like an announcement of death.

Scene 2

Lady Macbeth enters in a state of excitement. She has already made sure that the grooms are in a drunken sleep. She worries that people will awaken before Macbeth has killed the king. She would have killed him herself, she murmurs, except that he reminded her of her own father as he slept. Macbeth arrives, horrified at what he has done. In his fright he has brought the daggers with him instead of leaving them to incriminate the grooms. Because he has imagined a voice telling him he has murdered sleep and shall sleep no more, he cannot bear to go back into the king's chamber. Lady Macbeth goes to finish the deed for him. There is a sudden knocking at the gate, and Lady Macbeth returns to hurry her husband off to change into his night clothes so they can appear to be awakened. Lady Macbeth has had to take command because her husband is overcome with terror and remorse at what he has done and he imagines voices accusing him.

Scene 3

The knocking that ends the previous scene grows more insistent until a drunken porter enters to open the castle gate. He grumbles and curses whoever has awakened him, amusedly comparing himself to a porter at hell's gate and the arrivals as hoarders, equivocators, and cheats. Lennox and Macduff enter and are greeted by Macbeth. Macduff leaves to awaken the king and returns with a horrified announcement of the murder. Macbeth and Lennox go to see for themselves while Lady Macbeth and Banquo enter to hear the news from Macduff. By the time Macbeth and Lennox return, Donalbain and Malcolm have joined the others and Macbeth tells the sons that they must mourn their father. He also confesses to having killed the grooms in rage at having discovered their guilt in the murder of the king. Lady Macbeth faints, perhaps overcome by all that has gone on, or perhaps to deflect Macbeth from saying too much. In the stir created, the king's sons, Donalbain and Malcolm, slip away. They have decided that they will be safer in, respectively, Ireland and England.

Scene 4

Outside Inverness, an old man discusses with Ross all the strange omens of the past few days: an eclipse, a falcon killed by an owl, the king's horses turning wild and devouring each other. Macduff enters to inform them it has been decided the grooms killed the king, but it is suspected they did so on the orders of the king's sons. Their flight seems to support this suspicion. Macduff adds that the king is to be buried at Colmekill, and Macbeth is to be crowned at Scone. Macduff has decided not to attend the coronation but to return to his home in Fife. He hopes that Macbeth's rule will not be a harsh one.

ACT THREE

Scene 1

In the royal palace at Forres, Banquo wonders aloud what role Macbeth played in fulfilling the prophecies of the three witches. He also wonders if their prophecy for him will come true. Macbeth and his wife, now king and queen, enter and invite Banquo to a feast that evening. Banquo replies that he and his son Fleance are going riding but will return that night. When everyone else is gone, Macbeth summons two men whom he has convinced that Banquo has stood in the way of their success. He says he can't feel safe as king while Banquo lives and if the men have any courage at all they will get rid of Banquo who is their enemy, too. He tells them a way to kill both Banquo and his son when they return from their ride that evening, and the men agree to do so.

Scene 2

Lady Macbeth, although queen, hasn't found contentment. She sends for Macbeth and urges him to stop his solitary brooding. She tells him to be jovial among his guests that evening. Macbeth asks her to be especially attentive to Banquo that evening, and he hints that he has a plan for dealing with Banquo. That he does not tell his wife what he has in mind for Banquo and Fleance seems to indicate a breech between husband and wife. This is the first time in their plotting that he acts independently of her. He may merely want to present her with a deed accomplished, or he may feel he is in control now and need not consult her.

Scene 3

The two murderers, joined by a mysterious third person, wait in the park outside the castle for the return of Banquo and Fleance. When the returning riders dismount, the murderers attack them. Banquo manages to put up enough of a fight before being killed to give Fleance time to escape. The third murderer may be Macbeth himself or more likely some agent of his there to guide the other two.

Scene 4

Inside the banquet hall Macbeth is greeting his guests when one of the murderers arrives to report that Banquo is dead, but Fleance has escaped. Macbeth tries to take comfort that the greater danger of the two is disposed of. As the banquet continues, Macbeth has a vision of Banquo's ghost sitting in his place at the table. He addresses the ghost in terror, and Lady Macbeth soothes the guests by saying that her husband has been occasionally troubled by such fits since childhood. When the ghost leaves, Macbeth regains his composure and offers a toast to Banquo, but the ghost returns and Macbeth begins to rave. Seeing that she cannot calm him, Lady Macbeth asks the guests to leave. When they are gone, Macbeth complains to his wife that Macduff's failure to attend the banquet proves his disloyalty. Macbeth then declares he will again visit the three witches to learn what the future holds. Since only Macbeth had seen the ghost, it well may be a vision, like the dagger in Act 2, Scene 1, brought forth by his own guilt-ridden mind.

Scene 5

Hecate, goddess of witchcraft, scolds the three witches for talking to the ungrateful Macbeth without her guidance. She commands them to meet her at the pit of Acheron in the morning where she will raise artificial spirits to lead Macbeth to his doom. This scene adds nothing to the play and generally is thought to have been written by someone other than Shakespeare. The meter is different from the other witch-scenes, more sing-song, and the language not as fine. The song at the scene's end comes from Thomas Middleton's play *The Witch*.

Scene 6

Lennox and another lord back at Forres discuss the flight of Fleance, with Lennox adding ironically that now Fleance must be supposed guilty of his father's murder, just as Donalbain and Malcolm were accused of their father's death because they fled Scotland. It is clear from this conversation that Macbeth is suspected in the murders of both Duncan and Banquo. The lord explains that Macduff has gone to England to ask King Edward to support Malcolm against Macbeth. He adds his hope that the people of Northumberland and Siward will join in the fight to overthrow Macbeth and set Malcolm on the throne of Scotland. Word of these plans has reached Macbeth for, as the lord explains, he has begun to fortify his castle against attack. This scene may fit better in Act Four following Macbeth's visit to the three witches, but in either place it signals a change, a shift away from a series of successes for Macbeth and towards his eventual downfall.

ACT FOUR

Scene 1

The three witches meet around a bubbling cauldron into which they drop the loathsome ingredients of their spells: fenny snake, eye of newt, toe of frog, wool of bat, lizard's leg, and blindworm's sting. Hecate and three other witches join the three for a dance. These last leave as Macbeth enters to confront the original three and demand more prophecies. The witches conjure up three apparitions of his future. The first is an armed head that warns Macbeth to beware Macduff, (it is Macduff who later beheads Macbeth). The next is a bloody child who tells Macbeth he need not fear any man born of woman, (the child may signify Macduff who was "untimely ripped from his mother's womb," that is, born by Caesarian section rather than "born of woman" in the natural way, or it may be the young child of Macduff that Macbeth orders murdered). The last is a child crowned, with a tree in his hand, who proclaims that Macbeth shall never be vanquished until Birnam Wood comes to Dunsinane, (this is surely a portent of Malcolm's strategy of camouflaging his men with boughs of trees as they advance on the castle.) Macbeth, however, is reassured by these last two apparitions. Not willing to leave well enough alone, Macbeth demands to know whether Banquo's children will rule after all. Reluctantly, the witches produce a vision of eight kings, the last of them Banquo. Macbeth realizes that Banquo's descendants will rule Scotland. The witches dance and then vanish, leaving Macbeth to encounter Lennox who brings him word that Macduff has fled to England. Macbeth vows to himself to kill all of Macduff's family.

Scene 2

At Fife, Macduff's castle, Lady Macduff is complaining to Ross that her husband has left his family without protection. Ross tries to explain that Macduff had good reasons for his actions. He leaves, and Lady Macduff and her small son play a kind of game in which she tells him that his father is dead and a traitor, and he defends his father. A messenger enters and urges Lady Macduff to flee to safety, but she protests she has done nothing wrong. Macbeth's agents enter and after Lady Macduff refuses to say where her husband is, they kill her son, onstage, and pursue and kill her, offstage.

Scene 3

Macduff has gone to England to meet with Malcolm and urge him to overthrow Macbeth and take his rightful place as Scotland's king. Malcolm is suspicious of Macduff and thinks he may still be loyal to Macbeth. He thinks Macduff would hardly leave his family alone in Scotland if he did not enjoy Macbeth's protection. Macduff succeeds in convincing Malcolm at least to listen to him. To test him, Malcolm describes himself in unflattering terms, admitting to many vices and weaknesses. Macduff tries to minimize what he hears but finally has to protest that Malcolm isn't a worthy son to his good father. In fact, Macduff says of Malcolm, "Fit to govern? No, not to live." At this Malcolm confesses he was testing Macduff and assures him that he only wishes to serve his country well. Convinced of Macduff's loyalty, Malcolm tells him of the plans to join with ten thousand English troops under Siward in an invasion of Scotland. A doctor passes by and this prompts Malcolm to describe the curative powers of the saintly King Edward of England. This brief episode provides a sharp contrast between Edward and Macbeth. Ross joins the two men and after telling of the worsening situation in Scotland, he tells Macduff about the slaying of his wife and children. Macduff vows vengeance against Macbeth and the three men take their leave of Edward.

ACT FIVE

Scene 1

At Dunsinane Castle, one of Lady Macbeth's attendants describes to a doctor the queen's sleepwalking episodes. She is not willing to repeat what the queen says at these times, but asks the doctor to witness for himself what takes place. Soon Lady Macbeth appears, carrying a candle, and in her dream-state tries to wash an imaginary spot from her hand. In her mutterings are heard details of the deaths of Duncan and Lady Macduff. The doctor decides that her heart is overburdened with worry; she seems weak and broken in spirit. He advises the attendant to keep a close watch on her so that she doesn't harm herself. The doctor is so stunned by what he has seen and heard that he cannot speak of it. Lady Macbeth, who in Act 2 told her husband that a little water would wash away the blood from his hands, now cannot rid herself of the "filthy witness" to their deeds.

Scene 2

In the countryside near Dunsinane, Lennox, Angus, and other lords are gathered to meet Malcolm and the English forces. Macbeth, grown so savagely defiant that people consider him mad, has heavily fortified Dunsinane and awaits the attack of Malcolm's supporters.

Scene 3

When attendants bring Macbeth news of defections from his forces, he refuses to listen and clings to what he thinks is the protection of the witches' prophecies. The doctor arrives to tell Macbeth of his lady's deterioration. Macbeth urges him to find a cure for her, then he dons his armor and prepares for battle. Macbeth is virtually alone now. He can do nothing for his wife, and he seems reconciled to death if the battle is lost.

Scene 4

The Scots forces meet up with Malcolm and the English soldiers near Birnam Wood. Malcolm orders each man to cut off a tree branch and hold it in front of himself as camouflage when they advance on Dunsinane, thus ironically fulfilling the prophecy of the third apparition that Macbeth would never be defeated unless Birnam Wood moved against him.

Scene 5

Inside Dunsinane, Macbeth encourages the remnant of his forces by saying that the castle is so well fortified the attackers will starve before they can get in. Seyton brings Macbeth the news of the death of Lady Macbeth. Macbeth has so little emotion left, he hardly responds. The husband and wife who seemed so close in ambition and resolve are separated by death, and all Macbeth can do is comment on the futility of life. A messenger reports that the very woods seem to advance upon the castle. Macbeth now sees the duplicity of the third prophecy and determines at least to die "with harness on," that is, in his armor, in the field, fighting. He determines to leave the well-fortified castle.

Scene 6

When Malcolm's forces reach the castle itself, they throw down their tree boughs and prepare for combat. Malcolm is clearly in command, and for the first time, he uses the royal "we."

Scene 7

In the open field, Macbeth kills Young Siward, son of the English general, and in turn is pursued by Macduff. The castle falls, and most of Macbeth's remaining men desert him and fight for Malcolm. Macbeth keeps his courage up by reminding himself that he cannot be killed by any man born of woman.

Scene 8

At last Macbeth and Macduff meet face to face. Macbeth boasts that though Macduff may wound him, he cannot kill him. Macduff replies that the spirits Macbeth has served should have told him that Macduff was not of woman born but was, rather, untimely ripped from his mother's womb. Macbeth is dismayed when this last prophecy also proves deceptive. He refuses to fight Macduff. Macduff orders him to surrender and points out that the victors will humiliate him. Macbeth then renews the fight and cries, "Lay on, Macduff, and damned be him that first cries, 'Hold, enough!' " They exit fighting.

Scene 9

The forces gather around Malcolm to assess the battle. Ross brings Siward the news that his son was killed in battle. Siward accepts with a soldier's stoic resolve: "He died well and paid his debts. And so God be with him." Macduff enters with Macbeth's head and presents it to Malcolm. All hail Malcolm as king of Scotland. The new king announces his plan to make earls of his thanes and kinsmen—the first time this title has been used in Scotland. He invites all to his coronation at Scone. There is no gloating over the death and defeat of Macbeth, just a simple thank you from Malcolm to all who have served him so well.

QUESTIONS FOR DISCUSSION

ACT ONE

1. Why doesn't Duncan participate in the battle?

   COMMENT: Some students will say that because Duncan is king, he has others do his fighting for him. This idea can neither be proved nor disproved from the immediate context. But later on, when he is king, Macbeth participates in battle. And in other plays by Shakespeare, kings regularly fight in battles. Probably Duncan does not fight here because he is too old. Later on in the play, Lady Macbeth refers to Duncan as "the old man." But why is it important for students to have some idea of Duncan's age? Because it means that succession to the throne of Scotland is fairly imminent and that Macbeth must act soon if he is to realize his ambition.

2. In Scene 3 the witches plot revenge on the husband of a woman who has insulted one of them. The husband, a ship's captain, will have his vessel beset with storms, "though his ship cannot be lost," says the first witch. Why do you think she says this? Why can't his ship be lost?

   COMMENT: It is likely that here Shakespeare is setting a limit on the powers of the witches. They may cause a great deal of harm, but they can go only so far. If the witches had free-rein to do whatever they could, Macbeth would only be a pawn, robbed of the responsibility for his decisions, and this clearly is not what Shakespeare wants. Macbeth is not forced by the witches to kill Duncan; he is tempted.

3. Duncan waits until after the battle to announce his succession to the throne. Do you think Duncan is being shrewd? Would Macbeth and the others have fought as hard if they had known Malcolm was to be named the next king?

   COMMENT: Probably, Duncan is being shrewd, hoping to enlist the strongest support of Macbeth and Banquo. It is doubtful, however, that he is dangling the prospect of the crown before his generals. It's simply that they fight better to preserve a known present than an unknown future. What is more, he has good reason not to announce the succession of Malcolm before the battle is fought. If Duncan's forces lost, that would make Malcolm the target of the invaders. As for Macbeth and the others, they probably fought harder for Duncan than they would have for Malcolm. Their first loyalties, after all, were to Duncan.

4. We learn about characters in a play from what others say about them. We don't meet Macbeth until Scene 3. What kind of impression of him do we form before he first appears?

COMMENT: Naturally, our curiosity is aroused as we wait to see the protagonist of the play. The Captain says Macbeth deserves to be called brave. The king calls him valiant, worthy, and noble. We may feel a slight unease at Macbeth's seeming ruthlessness as he used his sword to cut Macdonwald open from navel to jaw. We may wonder if this is mere sword play in battle or a hint of cruelty to come.

5. The soliloquy is a playwright's device for allowing an audience to find out about a character. What do we find out about Lady Macbeth from her soliloquy when she calls on evil spirits to make her cruel and murderous enough to achieve her ambition?

COMMENT: This is our first glimpse of Lady Macbeth, and most people are shocked at how quick she is to respond to the news in Macbeth's letter with a plot of her own. She worries that Macbeth will be too mild to carry out her plan, so she decides to see that nothing gets in the way of his becoming king. She is even eager to seek help from the forces of evil to achieve her goals.

6. Why does Macbeth leave the banquet he has provided for Duncan?

COMMENT: He seems to be regretting the plot to kill the king or at least worrying about the repercussions after the murder. This serves to show Lady Macbeth that she may not be able to count on her husband to carry out their plan.

ACT TWO

1. Why does Macbeth have a vision of a dagger hanging before him?

COMMENT: He seems haunted by the murder he is about to commit. The weapon appears to him already dripping with blood as though the deed had been done. Perhaps he longs for it to be done without his having to act.

2. What is foreshadowed by Lady Macbeth's insistence that a little water will wash the blood from Macbeth's hands?

COMMENT: We later see that she is haunted by imaginary bloodstains on her hands and that her sleep is troubled with efforts to wash them clean.

3. The porter's monologue is often considered mere comic relief. Is it any more than that?

COMMENT: The language used and the imagery provided support the events of the play: hell gate, Belzebub, treason, stealing, devil-porter, and the grimmest image of all, the primrose path to the everlasting bonfire.

4. An Old Man and Ross discuss the unnatural events that have been taking place. What parallels with the murder of Duncan do these events offer?

COMMENT: The eclipse suggests the wiping out of the king. The owl killing the falcon shows a lesser creature overcoming a greater one. The cannibalism of the king's horses parallels Macbeth's murder of his own kind. The fourth event, the flight of the king's sons after supposedly hiring the officers to kill him, does not fool the audience, who know the real killers.

ACT THREE

1. Why does Macbeth feel threatened by Banquo?

   COMMENT: Banquo was with Macbeth when he heard the prophecy of the witches. Banquo is intelligent and may soon grow suspicious. Also, the witches predicted that Banquo was to be the father of kings. Since Macbeth has no son to succeed him, he wonders if he has done all this for Banquo's sons.

2. What change has taken place in the relationship between Macbeth and his wife?

   COMMENT: In the earlier scenes she did the planning and gave the instructions for Macbeth to carry out. What he failed to complete, she accomplished. In this act we learn that Macbeth has taken it upon himself to hire men to kill Banquo and his son Fleance. Furthermore, he has quite deliberately chosen not to tell Lady Macbeth of the deed until it's accomplished. As she tempers her first determination with hesitations and doubts, he grows more resolute in protecting what he has gained.

3. How are the hired killers able to kill Banquo so easily and yet allow Fleance to escape?

   COMMENT: Banquo and Fleance are walking from the stables to the castle itself so their cries would not be readily heard. Banquo seems to put up enough of a fight to occupy the murderers and so give Fleance the chance to escape, or at least he puts out the torch so that the killers can't immediately follow Fleance.

4. Once again Macbeth sees a vision, in this case Banquo's ghost. What can we infer about the state of Macbeth's conscience from this second vision?

   COMMENT: He is already so wracked with guilt that he no longer is able to act with discretion. At the banquet he speaks aloud before the assembled guests about the ghost he sees. He cries out that he is not responsible for Banquo's death. He carries on in a way sure to arouse suspicion. He is so distraught that he decides he must again seek the prophecies of the witches.

5. What purpose does the conversation between Lennox and the lord serve in this scene?

COMMENT: It provides exposition, allowing us to learn what the general public think of recent events. We also find out that Macduff has already gone to England to ask the help of the king against Macbeth.

ACT FOUR

1. What is the effect of the three prophecies on Macbeth?

COMMENT: He is encouraged by them. We, the audience, are alert to the ironic possibilities, but Macbeth takes the first prophecy, that Macduff is not trustworthy, as support of his own good judgement. The other two prophecies make him feel safe since both of them seem impossible: a man not born of woman? Birnam Wood moved to his castle? Surely, thinks Macbeth, these things can never happen.

2. How does the slaughter of Lady Macduff and her family affect us?

COMMENT: Although neither the murder of Duncan nor of Banquo was a deed a soldier could be proud of, the murder of Macduff's family is a gratuitous act of vengeful spite, and our sympathies shift entirely to Macduff.

3. Why does Malcolm describe himself as so steeped in vice that even Macbeth would seem pure as snow next to him?

COMMENT: He is testing Macduff's loyalty. Macduff, however, refuses to see any good in Macbeth. Macduff further assures Malcolm that any weaknesses he may have can be discreetly humored. Malcolm, able to trust Macduff, confesses that he has lied and actually he is innocent of vice and wishes only to serve his country well.

ACT FIVE

1. In Lady Macbeth's sleepwalking scene, with whom does she imagine herself in conversation?

COMMENT: She thinks she is talking with her husband and recalls what she said after Duncan's murder, the slaying of Banquo, Macbeth's behavior at the banquet, the murder of Lady Macduff, and the knocking at the gate the morning that Duncan's murder was discovered.

2. From the conversation among Monteith, Caithness, Angus, and Lennox, what do we learn about conditions at Macbeth's castle?

COMMENT: We find that the castle has been heavily fortified but that even those still with Macbeth are not loyal to him. Macbeth himself seems shrunk in stature so that his title hangs loosely on him. There is also a bit of exposition that helps account for characters that we haven't seen or heard of in a while.

3. How does Malcolm's plan of attack make a mockery of one of the witches' prophecies?

COMMENT: Malcolm cleverly has each man camouflage himself with a tree bough so that as they march on the castle it will bring Birnam Wood to Dunsinane.

4. What are Macbeth's feelings at the news of his wife's death?

COMMENT: He barely has time to wish she could have died at a later time when a messenger arrives to announce the horrifying news that Birnam Wood has begun to move upon Dunsinane. Macbeth does seem to be saying of his wife that her life and his life, life in general, has no purpose and ultimately means nothing.

5. What justice is there in Macduff being the one to kill Macbeth?

COMMENT: Although it is not a simple act of revenge, it is appropriate that Macduff be the one to kill Macbeth since Macbeth caused Macduff's family to be murdered.

6. What reward does Malcolm announce for those who loyally fought with him to defeat Macbeth?

COMMENT: They are to be earls, a title new to Scotland. This seems to signal a new order in the kingdom as well as showing that Malcolm is quick to thank those who helped him secure the crown.

7. Why is it important that Macbeth learn the falseness of the witches' guarantees? Wouldn't it be enough for the audience to know that the woods came to Dunsinane and that McDuff was delivered by Caesarian section? Why, do you think, Shakespeare wants the audience to know that Macbeth knows, too?

COMMENT: Shakespeare's play is not, strictly speaking, a history. It is the story of the effects of events on the emotions of Macbeth. Macbeth's reactions, not the events themselves, are the subject of the play.

STAGING MACBETH

There are four main locations in which a class might mount a production of *Macbeth*—in a proscenium arch auditorium, in an arena theatre, in a found space, or outdoors. Although some elements remain the same, each situation requires different considerations.

PROSCENIUM

In a proscenium arch auditorium, the audience usually expects a box set, rendered in as representational a manner as possible. Such a stage often allows for such tricks as trap doors through which the witches vanish suddenly, facilities for flying the witches in and out, and the use of a fog machine to create a murky atmosphere. But such an auditorium stage could also be decorated with just draperies and a few articles of appropriate furniture. A third method of scene setting would be to use a cyclorama and rear projection of such images as clouds, trees, and castle walls.

With a proscenium arch, it is also possible to use a scrim, a dark-blue theatrical gauze curtain, for some scenes, allowing for a quick change to the next scene with the mere lifting of the scrim. Having a front curtain means that some scenes—especially those brief scenes of conversation that provide exposition—can be played on the forestage in front of the curtain and a quick scene change can be effected by the raising of the front curtain to reveal the set behind it.

Taped atmospheric music, sound effects, and lighting effects are easily managed in the conventional proscenium arch auditorium as there are wings and back stage areas to work from. Such a situation also makes the changing of costumes and the arrangement of a properties table just off stage easy.

Of course, working on such a large stage has advantages and disadvantages in planning the blocking. There is room to stage battles, but there is also the need to "fill the stage" for such events as the banquet scenes and the arrival of the king and his entourage. If such a large cast is not possible, such scenes can be filled by asking the techies to don costumes and swell the processions. Also, when large numbers of actors are on stage together, they often may have to be reminded not to drift into a chorus line arrangement across the stage, but, rather, achieve groupings.

As modern editions of *Macbeth* divide the play into five acts, you will need to decide on the best place to pause for an intermission or two. More and more plays are being staged with just one intermission; it seems to work best for holding the interest of the audience at the performance until the end. A good place to break *Macbeth* is after Act 3, Scene 3. This is roughly the middle of the play so each act will be about the same length, but, more importantly, it will end the first act on a high note of horror, tension, and suspense: all the better to bring the audience back, eager for the second act.

ARENA

In an arena theatre, suggested scenery works best—that is, a group of tree cut-outs, some crafted rocks and boulders, banners and folding screens. Since there is no front curtain, the scene changes must be effected by the moving on and off of these scenery elements. This can be done by the "avista" method of having the stagehands in all black clothing working in 20 percent light. It is possible to use scrim at the rear of the fourth area, that not occupied by the audience, but there will not be much depth. It can, however, serve the same purpose as the "inner room" of the Globe Theatre's rear gallery. Some arena stages are sur-rounded completely by seating but it is possible, if you can afford to lose the income from a portion of seats, to block off a fourth of the circle and set up some kind of backdrop.

In such a location the tricks of trap doors, flying, and fog machines are not convenient. The fog machine should not be used close to an audience; you will have people protesting or coughing as the fog drifts.

Because there are no wings or backstage areas, arena stages usually have provisions for lighting and sound from a booth at the rear or side of the house. Facilities for the props table and any quick costume changes can be arranged behind the blocked off fourth area. Because the audience is so close to the actors, props need to be as realistic looking as possible. In some cases the blocked off area can even be hidden behind a cyclorama, making rear projection possible.Again, because the audience is so close, the battle scenes must be carefully blocked and the actors trained in techniques of stage combat. If this is not possible, productions have achieved good simulations of fighting by using actors in stylized motions on a darkened stage hit with a strobe light.

For asides and other solo speeches, the actors need to be trained to look into the middle distance rather than make eye contact with any audience members.The suggestion for an intermission, given in the section on proscenium arch staging, holds good here. And no matter what the location in which the play is staged, it's best to stick to a traditional version of the play. In all likelihood this is the first time the actors have performed *Macbeth,* and most of the audience may be seeing the play for the first time so there is no need to strain for novelty.

FOUND SPACE

When working in an indoor found space, be it cafeteria, classroom, or gymnasium, it's best to use suggested scenery. Unless you intend to rig up a curtain, any scenery changes will need to be effected by the avista method. Since the space is not commonly used for performances, you will need to figure out sightlines for the audience and arrange the seating accordingly. This also affects the blocking of the play. Several configurations may be possible: center staging, horseshoe arrangement of seats, bleachers at the front of your staging area, or dividing the room diagonally.

Lighting can be provided by light trees operated from the rear of the audience. A backdrop or screen at the rear of your playing area can provide a small backstage area for actors and props. The screen must be anchored securely as young actors making quick exits can easily knock it over.

As the audience is very close to the actors, props and costumes need to be as authentic looking as possible. But even in such close proximity, velveteen and waleless corduroy can look like velvet, and heavy polyester can pass for silk or taffeta. Colors can be used symbolically to add visual interest for the audience since they will not have a handsome set to admire.

As in arena staging, the solo speeches must be delivered to the middle distance and not directly to any audience member. Battle scenes present difficulties and a director in this situation may elect to keep such action off stage, narrated and further supported by sound effects.

Found spaces usually have built-in distractions: the basketball hoops in the gym, the serving counter in the cafeteria, the bookshelves in the library, the chalkboards in the classroom. Some things can be draped or screened; others kept out of sight by clever lighting plots. Even something as obtrusive as a serving counter in the staging area can be covered and used as the banquet table in *Macbeth*. There's no discounting the challenge the found space presents, but the rewards for inventiveness are highly enjoyable.

OUTDOORS

Speaking of challenges, don't be daunted at the prospect of using an outdoor space. Again, suggested scenery is the best bet, and a fog machine may work well. Light trees can provide adequate lighting, but music and sound effects may be too readily dissipated by the atmosphere and so need to be carefully rehearsed at the exact time of day or night the performances will take place. Then, too, the actors need to get used to projecting their lines in a less than resonant space.

As with the indoor found space, the sightlines will have to be calculated and seating arranged accordingly. If the audience will be seated on a lawn rather than on chairs, they may be restless and frequently change position. The actors need to realize this and not be disconcerted by it.

The distractions of an outdoor space range from cars, people, even animals passing by to insects and unexpected noises. While these may take the attention of the audience for the moment, actors who have been able to rehearse in the space and get used to its problems, can win the attention back again.

SELECTED BIBLIOGRAPHY

Beckerman, Bernard. *Shakespeare at the Globe 1599-1609.* New York: Macmillan Co., 1962.

> Covers such topics as the repertory performed at the Globe in that decade, the design of the stage, and the manner in which the plays were staged. Has an appendix with props lists for various Shakespeare productions.

Berman, Ronald. *A Reader's Guide to Shakespeare's Plays.* Glenview, Illinois: Scott Foresman, 1973.

> Provides a bibliography for each of the plays in such categories as Editions, Sources, Staging, and Criticism.

Bradbrook, M.C. *Themes and Conventions of Elizabethan Tragedy.* Cambridge: Cambridge University Press, 1964.

> The first half of the book deals with conventions of acting, speech, and action. There are references to twenty-four of Shakespeare's plays. The second half contains essays on the major dramatists of the period, such as Marlowe, Webster, and Middleton.

Bradley, A.C. *Shakespearean Tragedy.* Cleveland: World, 1964.

> Professor Bradley offers a series of ten lectures on *Hamlet, Othello, King Lear,* and *Macbeth.* In addition, a number of notes discuss such issues as whether Macbeth had any children, when Macbeth first had the idea of getting rid of Duncan, and how old Macbeth and Lady Macbeth are meant to be. An appendix, consisting of technical notes on the plays, takes up such items as the meter of *Macbeth,* whether Banquo's ghost is meant to be real or a hallucination, and when the murder of Duncan was first plotted.

Chambers, E.K. *Shakespeare: a Survey.* New York: Hill and Wang, 1958.

> Containing prefaces to all the plays, it was designed to help the "youthful beginner" approaching Shakespeare for the first time. The language is comprehendible and the tone unpatronizing. The preface to *Macbeth* sees the play as cosmic tragedy, that is, raised above the clash of ordinary good and evil to something exploring the whole mystery of temptation and retribution.

Clemen, Wolfgang. *The Development of Shakespeare's Imagery.* New York: Hill and Wang, 1951.

> Uses thorough examples to show the progressive stages of Shakespeare's imagery. The book is divided into sections on the Early and Middle Periods, the Great Tragedies, and the Romances. There is an exploration of the sleep imagery in *Macbeth.*

Coghill, Nevill. *Shakespeare's Professional Skills.* Cambridge: Cambridge University Press, 1965.

> One section, Visual Meaning, discusses such skillful theatrical devices as Lady Macbeth's sleepwalking and the witches' cauldron. There is also a section on the soliloquy.

Coles, Blanche. *Shakespeare's Four Giants*. Rindge, New Hampshire: Richard R. Smith Publisher, Inc., 1957.

> Contains separate essays on the characters of Hamlet, Macbeth, Othello, and Lear. The method is to concentrate on each of the four—excluding the other characters in the given play as much as possible.

Doran, Madeleine. *Endeavors of Art: a Study of Elizabethan Drama*. Madison: University of Wisconsin Press, 1964.

> Places the dramatists of the Elizabethan and Jacobean periods in the artistic context of their time. Covers such issues as art vs. nature, Aristotelian rules, and the debt to Roman comedy.

Dyer, Rev. T.F. Thiselton. *Folklore of Shakespeare*. New York: Dover, 1966.

> Explores Shakespeare's use of such folkloric elements as fairies, witches, and ghosts and such elements of nature as birds, plants, and insects. There are also chapters on rituals of baptism, marriage, and burial.

Fluchere, Henri. *Shakespeare and the Elizabethans*. New York: Hill and Wang, 1967.

> There is a foreword by T.S. Eliot recommending the book for relating Shakespearean drama to the other masterpieces of the Elizabethan theatre. Part One describes the spirit of the Elizabethan age. Part Two deals with techniques of characterization, conventions, and traditions. Part Three explores the major themes of Elizabethan drama and states that in the plays of Shakespeare we find the apotheosis of the age. The language is scholarly.

Knight, G. Wilson. *The Wheel of Fire: Essays in Interpretation of Shakespeare's Sombre Tragedies*. New York: Meridian Books, 1958.

> Contains essays on the tragedies *Hamlet, Othello, King Lear*, and *Macbeth*, with comments on a few of the other plays. Knight considers *Macbeth* to be a profound and mature vision of evil.

Robinson, Randal. *Unlocking Shakespeare's Language: Help for the Teacher and Student*. Urbana, IL: National Council of Teachers of English and the ERIC Clearinghouse on Reading and Communication Skills, 1989.

> Especially prepared for secondary and undergraduate college teachers, this publication addresses the problems most often encountered by beginning students of Shakespeare. Robinson draws on the contemporary and the colloquial to help students unravel such Shakespearean structures as inverted sentences, delayed constructions, and separations of related parts. Worksheets are included.

Spurgeon, Caroline. *Shakespeare's Imagery*. Cambridge: Cambridge University Press, 1975.

> Examines predominant images in Shakespeare in order to comment on the characters and themes of his plays. Some image clusters considered are those drawn from astronomy, sports, the sea, birds, food, medicine, and music.

APPENDICES AND GLOSSARY

Following are three appendices that you may wish to duplicate for your students. The Guide to Pronouncing Proper Names in *Macbeth* should probably be given to students at the beginning of the study of this play. (The terms in this guide are taken from the translation.) The same would hold true for the Shakespearean Time Line. It is useful to be reminded of the events of Shakespeare's life and how they fit into an overall historical framework. The two songs are sung by the three witches. These songs are referred to in the body of the text because they were probably part of the performance, but they are not printed there because they were not written by Shakespeare. They were written by his contemporary Thomas Middleton for his own play *The Witch*. The Glossary lists unfamiliar terms and place names with their definitions. The items in the Glossary are arranged alphabetically and references are given in parentheses to their use in the play.

APPENDIX I: A GUIDE TO PRONOUNCING PROPER NAMES IN *MACBETH*

Acheron	ĂK-ŭ-rŏn
Aleppo	ŭ-LĔP-ō
Angus	ĂNG-gūs
Banquo	BĂN-kwō
Beelzebub	bē-ĔL-zē-bŭb
Birnam	BĔR-nŭm
Caithness	KĀTH-nĕs
Colmekill	KŌM-kĭl
Duncan	DŬNG-kŭn
Dunsinane	DŬN-sĕ-NĀN
Fife	fīf
Fleance	FLĒ-ŭns
Glamis	GLÄM-ĭs
Golgotha	ĞOL-gō-thŭ
Gorgon	GÖR-gŏn
Hecate	HĔK-ŭ-tē *or* HĔK-ăt
Hyrcan	HĒR-kŭn
Inverness	ĭn-vĕr-NĔSS
Lennox	LĔN-ŭks

Lucifer	LŪ-sĭ-fĕr
Macbeth	măk-BĒTH
Macduff	măk-DŬF
Malcolm	MĂL-kŭm
Menteith	mĕn-TĒTH
Neptune	NĔP-tūn
Northumberland	nŏr-THŬM-bĕr-lŭnd
Ross	rŏs
Seyton	SĒ-tŭn
Siward	SĒ-ĕrd
Tarquin	TÄR-kwĭn

KEY: āce, ärm, ăt, ēve, mĕt, īce, hĭt, ōld, ŏx, ūse, ŭp

APPENDIX II: SHAKESPEAREAN TIME LINE

1557
Marriage of John Shakespeare of Stratford-upon-Avon to Mary Arden

1558
Accession of Queen Elizabeth

1564
Christening of William Shakespeare, the third child of John and Mary Shakespeare

1568
John Shakespeare becomes bailiff, or mayor, of Stratford

1576
First permanent theater built in London

1577-80
John Shakespeare experiences financial difficulties

1582
Marriage of William Shakespeare and Anne Hathaway

1583
Christening of Susanna, daughter of William and Anne Shakespeare, at Holy Trinity Church in Stratford

1585
Christening of Hamnet and Judith, twin children of Anne and William Shakespeare at Holy Trinity Church in Stratford

1588
Defeat of the Spanish Armada sent to invade England

1592
Shakespeare mentioned by Robert Greene as an actor and a playwright. London theatres closed because of plague

1593
Shakespeare publishes *Venus and Adonis*, a long narrative poem, based on poems by Ovid, and dedicated to his patron the Earl of Southampton

1594
London theatres reopened
Shakespeare becomes a member and a shareholder in the Lord Chamberlain's company of actors

1596
Hamnet Shakespeare dies

1597
Shakespeare purchases New Place, one of the largest houses in Stratford

1598
Francis Meres mentions "honey-tongued" Shakespeare as the author of twelve successful plays

1599
The Globe Theatre built and opened by Shakespeare's company

1601
John Shakespeare dies

1603
Queen Elizabeth dies, and James I ascends the throne
The Chamberlain's Men become the King's Men

1609
The Blackfriars Theater, in addition to the Globe, taken over by the King's Men

1610
Probable retirement of Shakespeare to Stratford

1616
Shakespeare dies at Stratford

1623
Publication of Shakespeare's collected plays, the First Folio

APPENDIX III: SONGS USED IN *MACBETH*

Come away, come away,

Hecate, Hecate, come away!

HECATE I come, I come, I come, I come,

With all the speed I may

With all the speed I may,

Where's Stadlin? (Act Three, scene 5, after line 33)

HECATE Black spirits and white, red spirits and gray,

Mingle, mingle, mingle, you that mingle may!

Titty, Tiffin,

Keep it stiff in;

Firedrake, Puckey,

Make it lucky;

Laird, Robin.

You must bob in.

Round, around, around, about, about!

All ill come running in, all good keep out! (Act Four, scene 1, after line 43)

(The Folger Concert plays *Shakespeare's Music,* including the two witches' dances of Macbeth; available from Delos Records, 2210 Wilshire Blvd., Suite 664, Santa Monica, CA 90403.)

GLOSSARY

The following terms are taken from this translation of *The Tragedy of Macbeth*. Act, scene, and line numbers are given in parentheses after the terms.

Acheron (act 3, scene 5, line 15): in Greek mythology, a river in the Underworld

adder's fork (act 4, scene 1, line 16): the forked tongue of a snake

Aleppo (act 1, scene 3, line 7): city in northern Syria

baited bear (act 5, scene 7, line 2): in Elizabethan times, bears were chained to posts and attacked by dogs for sport

Beelzebub (act 2, scene 3, line 3): one of the chief devils

bellman (act 2, scene 2, line 3): town crier who tolled a bell on the night before an execution

Birnam Wood (act 4, scene 1, line 102): a wooded hill about twelve miles from Dunsinane Castle in Scotland

blasted heath (act 1, scene 3, line 78): a flat, bare tract of wasteland, withered by storms and lightning

Colmekill (act 2, scene 4, line 42): small island, now called Iona, where Scottish kings were buried

curfew bell (act 3, scene 2, line 48): a bell sounded at evening

Evil, the (act 4, scene 3, line 165): scrofula; tuberculosis of the lymph nodes in the neck; it was believed that the king's touch could cure this disease

fell (act 4, scene 3, line 257): fierce, cruel

Fife (act 1, scene 2, line 54): area in eastern Scotland, site of Macduff's castle

Forres (act 1, scene 2, stage direction): site of the royal palace of Duncan, 11 miles southwest of Elgin, Scotland

Golgotha (act 1, scene 2, line 43): "place of the skull," where Christ was crucified

Gorgon (act 2, scene 3, line 74): a mythological creature whose glance turned people to stone

gray cat, demon toad (act 1, scene 1, lines 9-10): spirits embodied in animals that attend and serve a person

Hecate (act 2, scene 1, line 60): goddess of witchcraft and magic

hurlyburly (act 1, scene 1, line 3): uproar, tumult—of the battle described in the next scene

Hyrcan tiger (act 3, scene 4, line 118): a tiger from the ancient region of Hyricania, south of the Caspian Sea

incarnadine (act 2, scene 2, line 74): blood red

Inverness (act 1, scene 4, line 48): site of Macbeth's castle in northwest Scotland

lime (act 4, scene 2, line 39): a sticky substance smeared on branches to catch birds

Lucifer (act 4, scene 3, line 26): Satan's name before his fall

Mark Antony (act 3, scene 1, line 61): according to the Greek biographer Plutarch, Mark Antony was told by a fortune teller that his future would be darkened so long as he remained in the company of Octavius Caesar

Neptune (act 2, scene 2, line 72): the Roman god of the sea

parricide (act 3, scene 1, line 35): the killing of a parent

Roman fool (act 5, scene 8, line 1): commit suicide; Roman officers considered it honorable to kill themselves to avoid capture when defeated

Saint Colme's Isle (act 1, scene 2, line 69): an island in the Firth of Forth, a tidal mouth on the eastern coast of Scotland

Scone (act 2, scene 4, line 39): the ancient capital of Scotland

slowworm (act 4, scene 1, line 16): a small limbless lizard

Tarquin (act 2, scene 1, line 63): sixth-century Roman tyrant

thane (act 1, scene 2, line 49): a title of Scottish nobility, roughly that of an earl in England

twofold orbs and triple scepters (act 4, scene 1, line 132): symbols of sovereignty; the orbs here refer to England and Scotland; the scepters, to England, Scotland, and Ireland

untimely ripped (act 5, scene 8, line 20): prematurely delivered, by a Caesarean section operation

Weird Sisters (act 1, scene 3, line 32): sisters of fate or destiny; the three witches

Western Isles (act 1, scene 2, line 14): Ireland and the Hebrides, off the western coast of Scotland